C000129993

Bla Sketchbooks

London Adam & Charles Black

PUBLISHED BY
A. & C. BLACK · SoHo SQUARE · LONDON W.

OXFORD

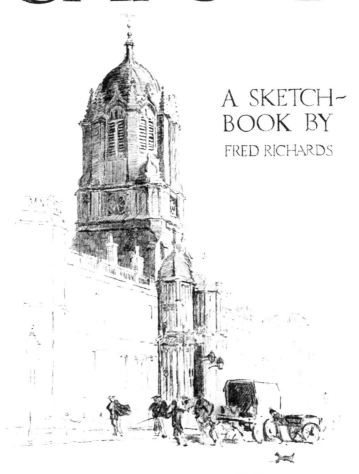

A SKETCH-
BOOK BY
FRED RICHARDS

A. & C. BLACK, LTD LONDON

LIST OF SKETCHES
by Fred Richards R.E.

THE HIGH
FROM TOP OF MAGDALEN TOWER.

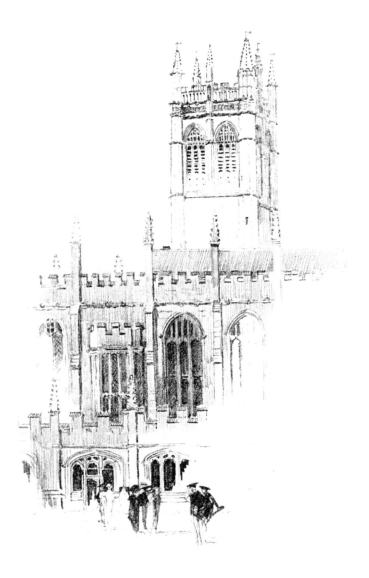

MAGDALEN COLLEGE   THE CLOISTERS

ST MARY THE VIRGIN (THE UNIVERSITY CHURCH)

QUADRANGLE & ENTRANCE TO DINING HALL. ORIEL.

THE CAMERA. FROM BRASENOSE COLLEGE.

BROAD ST

GREEK & LATIN ESSAY ROSTRUM   SHELDONIAN THEATRE   FCR

THE PORTER'S LODGE   TRINITY

A CORNER OF BALLIOL

THE DINING HALL   CHRIST CHURCH.

THE SUNDIAL
CORPUS
CHRISTI PER

A QUADRANGLE IN MERTON

THE RIVER FROM THE FOLLY BRIDGE

OXFORD FROM THE HINKSEY PATH.

First published in Great Britain in 1913
by A&C Black Publishers
36 Soho Square
London W1D 3QY
www.acblack.com

This edition published 2009

© 1913, 2009 A&C Black

ISBN 978-1-408-11555-8

A CIP record of this book is available from the British Library

Printed and bound in China